Liveryman and Grocer

A Letter to the Right Honourable Grocer

To which is prefixed, an essay on the origin of pensions in England.

Inscribed to a newly created baroness

Liveryman and Grocer

A Letter to the Right Honourable Grocer
*To which is prefixed, an essay on the origin of pensions in England. Inscribed to a
newly created baroness*

ISBN/EAN: 9783337195854

Printed in Europe, USA, Canada, Australia, Japan

Cover: Foto ©ninafisch / pixelio.de

More available books at **www.hansebooks.com**

A
LETTER
TO
The Right Honourable
GROCER.

TO WHICH IS PREFIXED,

An ESSAY on the ORIGIN of
PENSIONS in *England*.

Infcribed to

A Newly created BARONESS.

By a LIVERYMAN and GROCER.

———— " REM *facias* REM
" *Recte fi poffis, fi non, quocnnque modo* REM.

LONDON:

Printed for the Author; and Sold by I. POTTINGER,
in *Ave-Maria-Lane*, and at all the *Pamphlet-Shops*.

MDCCLXI.

AN
ESSAY
ON THE
Origin of PENSIONS.

E read in the moſt antient ſtates, that whenever a perſon diſtinguiſhed himſelf in the ſervice of his country, his grateful fellow-citizens were ſure to confer ſome public mark

mark of honour as a reward for his merit, and allowed particular privileges to him and his posterity.

The Romans carried this principle of patriotism to the greatest height; and we frequently find, in the infancy of the republic, that a parcel of oak leaves have been given to him who was fortunate enough to save the life of a fellow-citizen, as the greatest recompence of his heroism.

If a General was victorious, he was allowed a triumph, put into a certain vehicle, not much unlike our modern washing-tubs, and drawn through a crowd of admiring spectators, attended by a parcel of constables, ftables, who were alfo citizens and foldiers, but not then diftinguifhed by the appellation of train-bands; a fet of people who had no other advantage over the militia of thefe days, than the utmoft willingnefs to face their enemies.

A hot-headed chap, who had beat the Volfcians, was diftinguifhed by the name of Coriolanus; and in fucceeding ages, the title of Imperator was generally beftowed upon a fuccefsful Commander.

After the reduction of Britain by the Romans, and after we were beaten out of barbarifm by that civilized nation, we began to ftudy their language, and adopt their manners;

ners; for before the invafion, we
had no other diftinctions but two
words, which are at this day known
to fome people by the names of
Honour and Honefty. Honour was
the daughter of Honefty, begot by
Principle, and bred up by Virtue;
fhe was a young woman of fo pleafing an appearance, that fhe was fol-
lowed by the men, and copied by
the women; to be good was the
only nobility, and the different or-
ders of rank were proportioned to
the degrees of perfection.

Dr. Garth, in his Claremont,
very happily defcribes the manners
of our anceftors in thofe primitive
days of innocence and virtue. If

I

I do not very much miftake, he fays,

Of Spanifh red unheard of was the name,
For cheeks were only taught to blufh by fhame ;
Honour was plac'd in probity alone,
For villains wore no title but their own.

However, we began to adopt the cuftoms of our conquerors, and our patriots were not above receiving a proper mark of the public efteem for their fervices. An antient author, whofe name I have forgot, and it would not be of three halfpence fignification if I did not, fays, that a very great favourite of

C   the

the people was once prefented with a bunch of turnips, and the nobility, not to be outdone in generofity by their inferiors, unanimoufly voted him a leg of mutton, but made a provifo in the grant, that he fhould find butter and caper fauce himfelf.

But a fucceffion of ages produced a difference of thinking, and greatly polifhed the original rufticity of our manners; there was a neceffity for the invention of fomething to obtain the convenience of life, and a particular occafion to have it of fo portal a nature, that enemies of their country might receive a certain gratuity for the betraying the truft of the
people

people without being publickly dif-
covered, and univerfaily defpifed for
their corruption and venality : after
a good deal of confultation and de-
bate, we produced a fpecies of
coin in imitation of the Romans,
which has been handed down to
this day, and is now publickly
known by the name of money.

, Perhaps fome fenfible antiquarian
may remark, that our anceftors had
a number of coins before the invafion of the Romans, and that I
am very little acquainted with the
brafs or copper pieces of our pru-
dent forefathers; he is welcome,
fo he gives me leave to fay what I
pleafe; he may think what he

pleafes,

pleafes, and call me his very humble fervant.

From this invention of money, our nobility began to grow cold to the public intereft, and the commons weary of it; every man prudently confidered himfelf, and judicioufly thought his own welfare was his more immediate concern; fo that bunches of turnips, or legs of mutton, were no longer accepted by the great, or offered by the lower clafs of people. But the value of half a crown, or fo, was fure to make a nobleman, of the venal caft, as complaifant at that time, as it would now the footman of a man of quality after dinner.

The

The enemies of the conftitution, for the credit of thofe days be it faid, were not however the only perfons confidered: If a man had been remarkably ferviceable to his country, and a favourite of his Prince, he had the higheft mark of munificence from the one, and the moft pleafing addreffes of gratulation from the other---twenty fhillings a year was fettled upon him, perhaps for life, and he was allowed the firft cut at every public entertainment.

Thus we proceeded from age to age, ftill encreafing in the value of our penfions, till, in a late reign, a minifter received a greater falary

for

for difcontinuing to oppofe the hap-
pinefs of his country, than any
other perfon obtained for promot-
ing it.

A

A
LETTER
TO
The Right Honourable
GROCER.

A
LETTER
TO
The Right Honourable
GROCER.

On this foundation would I build my fame,
And emulate the Greek or Roman name:
Think England's peace bought cheaply with
  my blood,
And die with pleasure for my country's
  good.   ROWE.

DEAR BROTHER,

I F Mr. Rowe was juſt, in obſerving a real patriot ſhould die for the intereſt of his country, I fancy he might have alſo remarked, it would have

been

been much more neceſſary for him to have lived for it.

The Greeks and Romans were a little too haſty, in my opinion; for if, inſtead of falling upon the point of a ruſty ſword, they had perſevered in the reſiſtance they made to arbitrary meaſures, in all probability they might have happily ſucceeded, and reſtored their bleeding country to its original ſtate of tranquility.

Mr. Addiſon has put an expreſſion into the mouth of his Cato, wherein he ſays,

I ſhould have bluſh'd if Cato's
houſe had ſtood ſecure,
And flouriſh'd in a civil war.

By

By which we may underſtand, that that great man could by no means reconcile a deſertion of the public at the time they ſtood in moſt need of his aſſiſtance ; much leſs the ſmalleſt encreaſe of his fortune, as the purchaſe of forſaking them.

Different people, however, have different opinions ; and no man can take upon him to ſay how he would have acted in another perſon's place, unleſs he had in reality been in the ſame ſituation. Every man is undoubtedly the beſt judge of his own motives ; and if the uniform tenor of his conduct has been juſt and upright, a particular circumſtance

D 2   ſhould

should never make us change our
opinions, unless we are absolutely
convinced of his reasons.

Just, however, as this observation
may be, there are a multitude of
little minds generally busy in making
ill-natured strictures on the conduct
of their superiors, and take a malicious satisfaction of assigning any
reason for the seeming inconsistency
of their behaviour, but the real
one.

Difficult as it is to steer through
the channel of life without forfeit-
ing the esteem of the world, it must
certainly be a great consolation
to an ingenuous mind, to be convinced, that though he may have
incurred

incurred the difpleafure of the public by an extraordinary behaviour,
he is fortunate enough not to deferve it.

In public ftations, the characters
of the beft are liable to infpection;
and the more exalted the rank, the
more fevere the examination.

But when a man has done his utmoft in the fervice of his country,
when he has preferved her happi-
nefs, chaftifed her enemies, and
raifed her reputation, the moft en-
thufiaftic republican can by no means
fuppofe, but a proper concern for
the honour and welfare of his family fhould not be a very material
part of his concern.

Ay,

Ay, but fays a malicious world, ---might not the intereſt of his family been as well confulted by a continuance in the very employment by which he deferved fo fignal a mark of royal approbation, and by which he might likewife have an opportunity of receiving a ſtill greater token of regard?

Why, pray, what is that to the world?---fuppofe he thought proper to retire from bufinefs---fuppofe his health was impaired---fuppofe he wanted no further provifion for his family---fuppofe he was not pleafed at the refolutions taken with regard to the intended war with Spain, of the neceflity of which he

was

was abfolutely convinced---fuppofe any of thefe fuppofitions, and pray in what manner can his conduct be arraigned for making ufe of that freedom which the meaneft of the people imagine they have fo great a right to affert?---Is he not an Englifhman? has he not an un-doubted liberty of acting as he pleafes ? and fhould we not be thankful for the fervices he has done, inftead of being angry that they are not continued ?

Ay, but when the welfare of his country principally depended upon the abilities of a particular perfon, no other motive, no other confide-ration fhould be put in competition with it ; and the reigning principle

of

of every man fhould be, a regard for the intereft of the public.

Mighty pretty, truly ! the public are very much concerned about the intereft of itfelf; but why, in the name of common fenfe, fhould not individuals be equally follicitous about theirs? If this maxim is fo neceffary for the fafety of the community, why fhould it not be equally neceffary to private perfons? Let me afk one queftion---Does the general complaint of the behaviour of a certain great man, in his refignation, proceed fo much from what we may fuffer, as an agregate body; or does it principally fpring from the reafonable fear every fin-

gle

gle perfon may have of being affect-
ed himfelf.

Very consistent, indeed, that every body shall have a right of con-
fulting his own fatisfaction, but he,
who has the greatest title to every
indulgence.---Let me afk any one
perfon in the kingdom, if a plen-
tiful fortune was offered him for
life, for doing what his own incli-
nations might poffibly prompt him
to, if he would look upon himfelf
as bound in honour or duty to re-
fufe it?

Or if I have received a particular obligation from any body, inftead of that gratitude neceffarily
due on the receipt of a favour, would

E   it

it be reafonable to quarrel with a
friend becaufe he did not ftill think
proper to oblige me?

What has been faid with regard
to the concern of private people,
may, without impropriety, be ob-
ferved with refpect to public employments; though it muft be allowed, that the man who would pre-
ferve an opinion of his integrity,
fhould never give the leaft occafion
to fufpect it; and if there were any
particular reafons that might induce
him to an extraordinary method of
acting, the juftice due to his own
character fhould oblige him to de-
clare them.

Not-

Notwithſtanding that motive for an explanaticn of his conduct, there is ſtill a juſtice due to the community, which the greateſt of its members have a right to obſerve, and from which no conſideration in nature can poſſibly diſcharge them.

This duty is ſtill more incumbent on thoſe perſons who have voluntarily accepted of employments, where the general intereſt is materially concerned, and who have more noble opportunities of conſulting the welfare of the public ; and if they have accepted of thoſe places with chearfulneſs, have a right to diſcharge them with honour.

From

From thefe confiderations there-
fore, brother, though every man in
fome particulars has a right to the
difpofal of his abilities, or the employment of his time; yet this is
one of the circumftances where no
excufe can poffibly acquit him.

The pilot would have but a poor
excufe for leaving a veffel in a dan-
gerous channel, becaufe it was the
general opinion of the crew it was
not fafe to venture through it, tho'
he himfelf, from ftudy and experi-
ence muft be well convinced of the
practicability.

Ill grounded as popular complaints
may generally appear, yet upon the
prefent

prefent fubject, the kingdom cannot but greatly regret the lofs of thofe abilities which have added fo much to its reputation, and the juft opinion that was conceived of them needs no other proof than the general diffatisfaction.

When we had the greateft hopes, by a proper exertion of talents fo fuperior, to fcourge the infolence of our perfidious enemies, and to fix an honourable and advantageous peace, to be deprived of them, muft be a matter of real concern to every well-wifher of his country; more efpecially as the enemies of the public favourite are but too ready to encourage fufpicions not greatly to the honour of his character.

For

For this reason we cannot help lamenting the fatality of those circumstances which deprived us of so faithful and able a minister, and wish we could make his enemies believe the real cause of his resignation were the motives publickly assigned.

For our own parts, we are fully satisfied with his conduct, and sincerely applaud his resolution in the quitting an employment he was not allowed any longer to conduct with reputation to himself, or with credit to the nation ; we are highly sensible of the greatness of his services, and shall ever remember them with the deepest gratitude.

Con-

Confcious of the injuftice done to the beft of characters, we are only concerned that appearances are faid to make againft it; and fenfible of the greatnefs of his integrity, we are forry any perfon can be bafe enough to fufpect it.

The fpontaneous marks of royal munificence, we are affured, were never more happily difpofed; and we are convinced, no perfon was more properly calculated to deferve them.

A world, naturally cenforious, will embrace every opportunity of blackening the name of merit; and it is with the utmoft anxiety we ob-
ferve,

ferve, the greateft number of the people take . hold of this occafion.

From the impoffibility of removing public prejudices without a public vindication, the neceffity of this letter will fufficiently plead its excufe: the author is happy if he can be in the leaft inftrumental in juftifying a name he muft always admire; or in recovering an individual from the error of an opinion founded alone upon calumny and ill-nature.

He would gladly wifh a more able pen had undertaken the defence of a character fo feverely treated; and cannot again help declaring

claring his concern for fo great an
inftance of ingratitude.

But time, he is convinced, will
make every body well acquainted
with his motives, and fhew how far
the affertions of his enemies have
been juftly grounded.

POST-

POSTSCRIPT.

AS in the courfe of the foregoing letter, no reafons have been given, either in regard to the neceffity of a Spanifh war, or the expediency of continental connexions; it may be proper, in this place, to give the opinion of the public upon a fubject which has already, moft worthy Brother, been honoured with your own.

F 2   You

You are undoubtedly right, in af-
ferting, that the infolence of the
Spaniards, in prefuming to meddle
in a general pacification, or in ap-
pearing the profeffed friends of
our prefent enemies, fhould be feverely fcourged for that, will not
only enhance the reputation of the
kingdom, and provide a mainte-
nance abroad for a number of people who could not poffibly exift at
home, but give the nation an opportunity of throwing away fome
thoufand burthenfome lives, and
unneceffary millions of money with
which fhe is already pretty much
incumbered : befides, had a certain
refignation not happened, the public would have the greateft room to
fhew

shew their regard to a Right Hon. Perfonage, by their readinefs in fub-fcribing any confiderable fums for which there could not be the fmalleft occafion.

With refpect to continental connexions, you are moft certainly right; the Englifh nation has been, for a long time, as much diftinguifhed for its generofity, as eminent for its valour; and it certainly is the bufinefs of every lover of his country, to omit no opportunity of exercifing either. The lefs our intereft is advanced by our German connexions, the more our generofity is raifed; and the more lives that are loft, in defence of a country with which England has no manner of concern, the

the more she enhances her character of bravery.

Let it be the business of other kingdoms to engage in wars from principles of found policy and government ; but let it be our's to proceed from no other motives but a real regard to the interest of our friends, and a generous inattention to our own.

From this it must evidently appear, that the commencement of a Spanish war, and the continuation of a German one, are essentially necessary to the preservation of our national characteristics ; and that every real lover of his country should with-

withdraw from any employment, in which he was not allowed to profecute the one with fpirit, and continue the other with vigour.

F I N I S.

www.ingramcontent.com/pod-product-compliance
Lightning Source LLC
Chambersburg PA
CBHW021448090426
42739CB00009B/1682